All-Terrain Sports

Andrew Luke

MASON CREST

Adventurous Outdoor Sports Series

Air Sports

All-Terrain Sports

Mountain Sports

Snow Sports

Water Sports

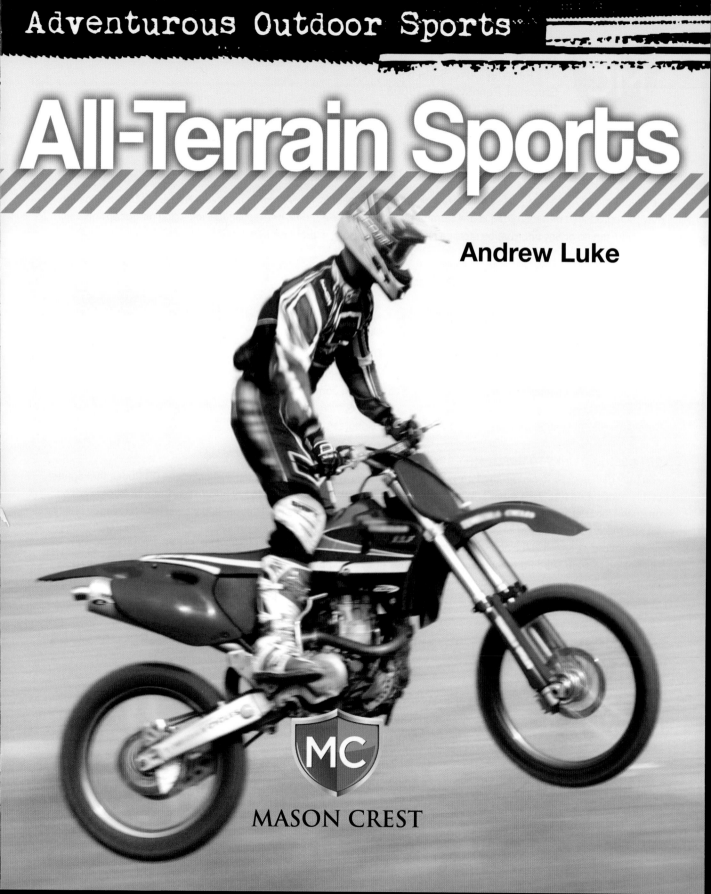

Adventurous Outdoor Sports

All-Terrain Sports

Andrew Luke

MASON CREST

MASON CREST

450 Parkway Drive, Suite D
Broomall, Pennsylvania 19008
(866) MCP-BOOK (toll-free)

Andrew Luke

First printing
9 8 7 6 5 4 3 2 1

ISBN (hardback) 978-1-4222-3706-9
ISBN (series) 978-1-4222-3704-5
ISBN (ebook) 978-1-4222-8079-9

Cover and Interior designed by Tara Raymo; www.creativelytara.com

Cataloging-in-Publication Data on file with the Library of Congress

QR CODES AND LINKS TO THIRD-PARTY CONTENT
You may gain access to certain third-party content ("Third-Party Sites") by scanning and using the QR Codes that appear in this publication (the "QR Codes"). We do not operate or control in any respect any information, products, or services on such Third-Party Sites linked to by us via the QR Codes included in this publication, and we assume no responsibility for any materials you may access using the QR Codes. Your use of the QR Codes may be subject to terms, limitations or restrictions set forth in the applicable terms of use or otherwise established by the owners of the Third-Party Sites. Our linking to such Third-Party Sites via the QR Codes does not imply an endorsement or sponsorship of such Third-Party Sites, or the information, products, or services offered on or through the Third- Party Sites, nor does it imply an endorsement or sponsorship of this publication by the owners of such Third-Party Sites.

Table of Contents

Key icons to look for:

Words to Understand: These words with their easy-to-understand definitions will increase the reader's understanding of the text while building vocabulary skills.

Text-Dependent Questions: These questions send the reader back to the text for more careful attention to the evidence presented there.

Sidebars: This boxed material within the main text allows readers to build knowledge, gain insights, explore possibilities, and broaden their perspectives by weaving together additional information to provide realistic and holistic perspectives.

Research Projects: Readers are pointed toward areas of further inquiry connected to each chapter. Suggestions are provided for projects that encourage deeper research and analysis.

Educational Videos: Readers can view videos by scanning our QR codes, providing them with additional educational content to supplement the text. Examples include news coverage, moments in history, speeches, iconic sports moments and much more!

The World of All-Terrain Sports

Rocks. Sand. Snow. Gravel. Shallow creeks. Mud. Each of these is an example of a type of surface an all-terrain sport may take place on. Whether it be with bicycles, motorcycles, trucks, cars, or ATVs, people have been racing their vehicles off the beaten path for decades and have continued to choose that more rugged, unpaved path even after speed seekers turned to smooth surfaces.

All-terrain enthusiasts prefer the added element of danger presented by a track that fights against them or the adrenaline rush of soaring and twisting high above that track.

Dune bashing, green laning, mudding, and rock crawling are just a few examples of all-terrain sports. All-terrain drivers will compete on just about any surface, from ice and snow-covered slopes (the Frozen Rush) or scorching desert sand (the Baja 500) to the inside of an empty swimming pool or the railing on a flight of stairs.

Michigan-born Walker Evans won more than 140 races in his Motorsports Hall of Fame career. A star of racing on short-course dirt tracks, he also made his mark on long-haul races from 250 to 1,000 miles (402 to 1,609 kilometers) through the deserts of Mexico, Las Vegas, and Arizona. Evans was a pioneer on the sand in the 1970s, just as Gary Denton was racing ATVs in the 1980s and Terry Tenette in BMX in the 1990s. These stars and their peers set the stage for the dynamic array of all-terrain sports that has developed in the 21st century.

Mountain Biking

Downhill MTB is considered to be the most dangerous form of the sport.

 Words to Understand

air suspension: a compressed air shock absorption system that improves control, traction, and comfort of riders over rough terrain.

employ: to make use of.

exploits: notable deeds or feats, especially ones that are noble or heroic.

Off-road bicycling has been around since the late 19th century, and French and English riders developed bikes specially modified or constructed for riding on rough, uneven terrain in the mid-20th century.

It was in the mid- to late 1970s, however, that the modern sport of mountain biking (MTB) emerged. Teenagers in California began modifying their Schwinn bikes equipped with balloon tires (wide, low-pressure tires) around the hills in Marin County. Their **exploits** started a craze that spread around the region as riders began stripping and modifying bikes to handle off-road terrain. Manufacturers took note and began to redesign the bikes themselves, and by the 1990s all makers were building bikes designed for the booming sport of MTB.

Downhill MTB courses can contain 40-foot (12 meter) jumps and 10-foot (3 meter) drops.

There are two main types of MTB: downhill and cross-country. As the name indicates, the terrain for the sport of downhill MTB can be summarized in one word: steep. Riders use heavy bikes with front and rear **air suspension**, carbon fiber parts, big disc brakes, and tubeless tires. Riders start at the top of a course that includes 40-foot (12 meter) jumps and 10-foot (3 meter) drops over extremely rough terrain. Downhill is considered the most dangerous type of MTB riding.

In cross-country MTB, riders use bikes that are about 15 lbs. (7 kilograms) lighter than downhill bikes. They are designed for point-to-point riding across varying terrain with both climbs and descents. Cross-country is the most popular form of MTB and the only one that is represented at the Olympic Games. Cross-country races generally **employ** a mass start, with the first to cross the finish line declared the winner. Downhill races are timed.

Cross-country MTB is the most popular form of the sport.

 ## Sidebar

Recreational mountain bikers tend to stick to the cross-country version of the sport. The competition version of MTB is often portrayed in media coverage as high speed and dangerous. In fact, the great majority of riders engage in MTB for the exercise and the tranquility of a scenic ride that allows them to clear or focus their minds. Most people that are attracted to the sport are not looking for an adrenaline rush.

While most mountain bikers are not looking to risk life or limb, MTB is still beyond the normal concept of a leisure activity. Serious enthusiasts come in three main groups. There are those that are outdoor lovers. MTB is just another avenue to explore their passion for the outdoors. Another group of MTB riders are the cycling junkies. A lot of road cyclists found the sport while looking for a change in the way they experienced riding. Then there is the group of riders who just love MTB on its own. They typically do not participate in other outdoor activities, and many have not ridden since childhood before stumbling across MTB. The new interest may have come from choosing a day renting mountain bikes as a vacation activity to the enthusiastic recommendation of friends who described the positive effects the sport had on their lifestyle.

Text-Dependent Questions

1. When did the modern sport of MTB emerge?
2. What are the two main types of MTB?
3. What kind of start is commonly used for cross-country MTB races?

Research Project

Compare and contrast the equipment needed for cross-country versus downhill MTB. Be sure to include protective equipment as well as bicycle types in your analysis.

Cross-country bikes are lighter than those used for downhill and are designed for use over varying terrain, including hills and creek beds.

Educational Video

Scan here to see MTB in action.

BMX

Bicycle motocross is held on courses designed with dips and jumps, where up to eight riders battle to be first across the finish line.

Words to Understand

emulating: imitating with effort to equal or surpass.

sanction: to give authoritative permission or approval, as for an action.

simulate: to create a likeness or model of a situation or condition.

BMX stands for bicycle motocross, and its name comes from the motorcycle event it started out **emulating**. At about the time their northern California counterparts in Marin County were taking their bicycles off-road, teenagers in southern California began taking their own Schwinn models to race on dirt tracks that had been built for motorcycle racing, or motocross.

The dirt tracks were built with dips and jumps to **simulate** uneven terrain, and by 1974, the thrill of racing on these courses spread to the East Coast with the formation of the National Bicycle League in Florida. The American Bicycle Association followed soon after in Arizona in 1977. Both **sanction** BMX events in the United States today.

By 1981, the sport was international, and the International BMX Federation was founded, with World Championships held the next year. BMX became mainstream in 1993, when it was recognized by the Union Cycliste Internationale (UCI), or International Cycling Union in English, the Swiss-based governing body of cycling. BMX became an Olympic medal sport in 2008.

Racers are grouped by two wheel size classes (20 or 24 inches [50 or 61 cm]) and by age or experience level within each class. Competitions include several heats (called Motos) that determine the eight riders for the final (the Main).

Professionals race on the USA BMX Pro Series, an 11-month-long circuit with more than 25 events. Top BMX pros include Australian Sam Willoughby and Minnesota's Alise Post.

BMX racing was an international craze by the early 1980s. The race shown here took place in Norway, one of dozens of countries where the sport is popular.

Competitions consist of Motos (heats). Doing well in the Motos gets riders to the Main (final).

Sidebar

Gabriela Diaz of Argentina is the most decorated woman ever to race BMX. She is a three-time elite category UCI world champion, winning gold medals three times in 4 years from 2001 to 2004. She has seven UCI medals in total. Diaz also holds six Pan American championship titles and a gold medal at the 2007 Pan American Games.

Text-Dependent Questions

1. What does BMX stand for?
2. What year was the National Bicycle League founded?
3. What are the two wheel size classes in BMX?

Research Project

Check out a BMX track near you, and investigate the steps needed to sign up to learn, practice, and compete in BMX.

Educational Video

Scan here to watch a BMX rider.

Freestyle BMX

Freestyle judges are looking for difficulty and creativity in the tricks riders perform.

 Words to Understand

brethren: fellow members.

emerge: to come forth into view or notice, as from concealment or obscurity.

pivot: a pin, point, or short shaft on the end of which something rests and turns or upon and about which something rotates or oscillates.

While some kids took to racing the new purpose-built BMX bikes in the 1970s, others found a whole new way to use them. Instead of seeing how fast they could go, these kids wanted to see how much they could control the bikes.

Californian Devin Bank is often credited as being the first kid who tried to make his BMX bike do something it wasn't designed to do. His brother Todd took a photo of Devin in 1974 attempting to spin his BMX bike at the top of a skateboard ramp using its rear wheel as a **pivot**. Freestyle BMX riding was born.

For the rest of the 1970s, kids like Devin and Todd followed their skateboarding **brethren** to empty swimming pools and then to skate parks, doing tricks on their bikes like skaters did on their boards.

In BMX, riders compete doing tricks in skate parks, like this one off a tabletop feature.

Sidebar

Sports network ESPN's X Games is the top level of competition for freestyle BMX. One of the greatest BMX riders of all time was freestyle legend Dave Mirra. The upstate New York native won 23 X Games medals in freestyle BMX, including 14 gold. Mirra won the Park Competition 5 years in a row from 1996 to 2000. At the 2000 X Games, Mirra became the first rider to ever land a double backflip in competition.

One of the first freestyle innovators to **emerge** from the Los Angeles scene onto a national stage was David "Tinker" Juarez. Juarez started racing BMX in 1974 and won the very first Grand National BMX Championship the next year at just 14 years old. Juarez was also a BMX wizard off the ground as well, spending so much time perfecting tricks on his BMX that *Bicycle Motocross Magazine* put him on the cover, soaring off a vertical bowl in 1980 with the title "King of the Skate Parks." Freestyle exploded in popularity in the 1980s, as did freestyle competitions, which are won by the rider judged to have performed the best tricks.

Several styles developed over the years, including these:

- Dirt – also known as Trails, riders follow a dirt circuit containing several ramps off which airborne tricks are performed
- Flatland – riders perform tricks while riding on flat, smooth surfaces
- Park – these riders get air doing jumps and perform tricks in skate parks
- Street – originally born of doing tricks using items found on any city street, such as rails, curbs, stairs, ledges, and so on
- Vert – riders use a half pipe to launch themselves vertically into the air above it to perform tricks like tailwhips, Supermans, and fakies

Flipping the bike while airborne is a standard freestyle trick.

  **Text-Dependent Questions**

1. Who was the first to use his BMX bike to do a trick?
2. Who was dubbed "King of the Skate Parks" in 1980?
3. Name three tricks performed in BMX Vert.

 Research Project

Create a timeline highlighting key moments in freestyle BMX history. Investigate pioneers such as Dave Mirra, Ryan Nyquist, and Mat Hoffman, and progress to the feats of Garrett Reynolds, Dennis Enarson, Jamie Bestwick, and beyond. Along with key moments from the sport's origins, also include at least two key developments or accomplishments in each decade from the 1970s to now.

Freestyle genres include street, which uses rails, fences, and curbs as props, and vert, which is all about getting big air out of a half pipe.

Educational Video

Scan here to see freestyle BMX.

ATV

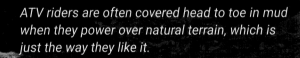

ATV riders are often covered head to toe in mud when they power over natural terrain, which is just the way they like it.

 Words to Understand

amphibious: able to be used both on land and water.

enthusiasts: people who are filled with zeal for some principle or pursuit.

modification: the act or process of changing parts of something.

An ATV is an all-terrain vehicle. The term typically applies to three- or four-wheeled vehicles with low-pressure tires that are straddled by the rider and steered with handlebars, like a motorcycle would be.

Originally designed as **amphibious** military vehicles, the modern versions were introduced in the 1960s, beginning with the three-wheeled models. These early models were not truly all-terrain, however, as they lacked suspensions. In the 1980s, Japanese manufacturer Honda introduced three-wheelers with racks and suspensions, and these soon became the go-to vehicles in rural areas of North America for getting around the ranch or farm to making it possible to get to that favorite fishing or hunting spot.

In the mid-1980s, the four-wheeled models were introduced. These were intended to be higher-performance recreational vehicles, had more power and better suspensions, and were lighter as well. **Enthusiasts** soon realized that with a few **modifications**, these were racing machines.

ATV racing has developed as a motorsport internationally, as these racers in New Zealand demonstrate.

The Grand National Cross Country circuit, which started in the mid-1970s as an off-road motorcycle racing series, added ATVs in the mid-1980s. It now runs a 13-event series, each featuring a 2-hour ATV race for the pros as well as amateur races with ages classes as young as 4 years old.

The ATV MTX National Championship series started in 1985. The 12-round series currently runs from March to September at motorcycle parks and tracks from Daytona, FL, to Mount Pleasant, MI.

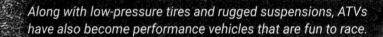
Along with low-pressure tires and rugged suspensions, ATVs have also become performance vehicles that are fun to race.

Sidebar

There are several different kinds of ATV racing. These include variations on cross-country, motocross, sand or dune racing, ice racing, and speedway events. One of the most familiar varieties is mud racing. Racing through the woods during the rainy season and emerging splattered head to toe with mud is a common weekend pursuit for ATV lovers. In 2006 it became a regulated series like all the others.

 **Text-Dependent Questions**

1. What does ATV stand for?
2. When were four-wheeled ATVs introduced?
3. When did the ATV MTX National Championship series start?

 **Research Project**

Investigate how old you need to be to legally operate an ATV in the United States. Does it vary from state to state versus federal law, and if so, why do some states allow these differences?

 **Educational Video**

Scan here to watch an ATV adventure.

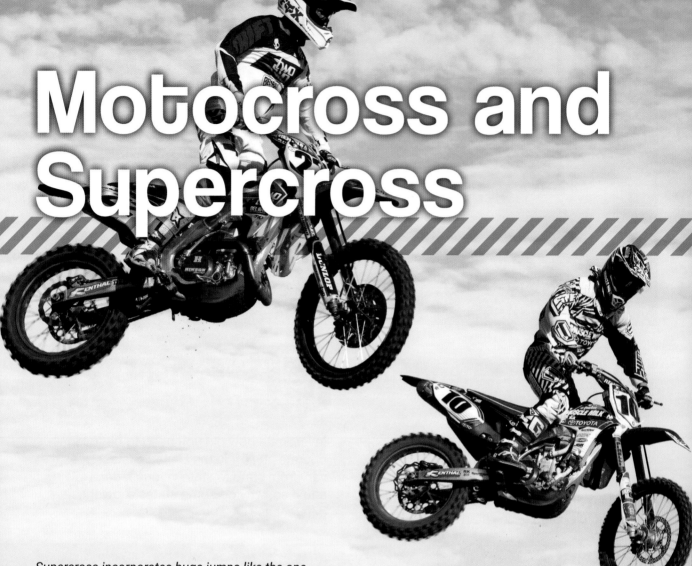

Motocross and Supercross

Supercross incorporates huge jumps like the one that sent these two racers soaring through the air.

Words to Understand

evolved: changed or developed slowly often into a better, more complex, or more advanced state.

prominence: the state of being important, well-known, or noticeable.

suitable: having the qualities that are right, needed, or appropriate for something.

Motorcycle racing has been around since the late 19th century. In early 20th-century Britain, it was known as "scrambles racing" and involved racing street motorcycles cross-country over rugged terrain. The sport became popular, leading to the demand for more **suitable** bikes. English manufacturer Birmingham Small Arms developed off-road motorcycles with suspensions and dominated the market and racetracks with big, heavy machines through the 1950s.

The mass start at an AMA Supercross race in Atlanta, GA, ensues.

In the 1960s, the sport, by this time commonly known as motorcycle cross or motocross (motorcycle and cross-country) had two major developments. First, new engine technology allowed for smaller and lighter engines that allowed Japanese manufacturers to gain **prominence.** Second, motocross was introduced to the United States in 1966.

Motocross was a huge hit in America, drawing big crowds to arenas and even stadiums. In 1972, the Super Bowl of Motocross was held at the Los Angeles Coliseum, which seats more than 80,000 people. Modern motocross racing includes a combination of natural terrain and man-made obstacles and is run on an outdoor track with several riders competing in two races where they earn points based on where they finish. The rider with the most points after two races is the winner, even if he or she did not actually win either race.

Supercross racing **evolved** from motocross. Supercross now starts the off-road racing season, with the pros competing in 17 races starting in January (they switch over to motocross in the second half of the year). Supercross takes place indoors in arenas or stadiums on 100 percent man-made courses with lots of high jumps, curves, and turns. There is a single 20-lap race, and the winner is the rider who crosses the finish line first.

After originating in early 20th-century Britain, motocross expanded across the globe. This racer is competing in the Fabrichny Cup Open Championship in Kazakhstan.

Sidebar

San Francisco-born Jeremy McGrath is known as the "King of Supercross," and he was pretty good at motocross as well. When McGrath retired (for the second time after a 2-year comeback attempt) in 2006, he had racked up 72 American Motorcyclist Association (AMA) Supercross wins and 17 AMA National Motocross wins. He was AMA Supercross champion seven times, including in 1995, the year he also won the Outdoor Motocross Championship. He was inducted into the AMA Motorcycle Hall of Fame in 2003.

Text-Dependent Questions

1. When was motocross introduced to the United States?
2. Which takes place indoors, motocross or Supercross?
3. How many laps are there in a Supercross race?

Research Project

Examine the differences between Supercross and motocross. List three skills that allow riders to excel in each discipline, and explain why.

Racers battle for position in the first turn of an AMA Motocross Pro National event in New Berlin, NY.

Educational Video

Scan here to see motocross in action.

Enduro

Enduro courses can contain man-made obstacles, like these half-buried cable drums.

Words to Understand

factored: included as an essential element.

grueling: exhausting, very tiring, arduously severe.

stout: strong of body, hearty, sturdy.

Motocross and Supercross bikes, although equipped with good suspensions to handle jumps, are built for speed. That is especially true when compared to enduro bikes. Enduro, as the name indicates, is an endurance test against the clock that presents motorcycle riders with several obstacles and challenges. Enduro bikes have **stout** suspensions and bigger gas tanks than motocross machines. This is essential as the terrain is the primary challenge. Riders must go over logs and under tree branches, race up rocky hillsides and down muddy slopes, and deal with a variety of man-made obstacles as well.

Traditionally, enduros begin with riders leaving in groups at timed intervals. The course is set up in such a way that riders are expected to hit certain points at predetermined times after their start time. They are penalized for being either too early or too late. The winner has the fastest time after penalties are **factored** in.

In the United States, the Grand National Cross Country (GNCC) circuit runs a 13-event season and is the most popular enduro series. Races are typically 3 hours long. There is also the Full Gas Sprint Enduro series, which runs eight **grueling** events from February through November.

Internationally, the biggest enduro event is the World Enduro Championship, sanctioned by motorcycle racing governing body FIM. The format includes eight 2-day events, which include not only an enduro test but an extreme test and a motocross test as well.

The oldest enduro event is the International Six Days Enduro (ISDE), which has been contested since 1913. This team event takes place at different venues around the globe every year and covers more than 1,250 miles (2,012 kilometers) over 6 days.

Enduro bikes have excellent suspensions that allow them to handle challenging obstacles.

Sidebar

Juha Salminen of Finland is one of the most successful enduro riders in the sport's history. He won the World Enduro Championship overall title 5 years straight, from 2000 to 2004. Salminen added the class E1 (125 cc two-stroke engine) title in each of 1999, 2007, and 2011 as well, for a record eight world titles. He was also instrumental to his country's success at the ISDE, leading Finland to six ISDE World Trophies, including a win on home soil in 2011. Salminen is also a two-time GNCC champion.

Text-Dependent Questions

1. Name two differences between motocross bikes and enduro bikes.
2. How many events are there on the GNCC enduro circuit?
3. When was the first ISDE held?

Research Project

Investigate and explain the difference between a two-stroke and four-stroke engine. What are the advantages of each in motorcycle racing?

Educational Video

Scan here to see enduro.

Trials

Trials do not involve racing. Trials drivers are striving for precision and control.

Words to Understand

infractions: breaches, violations, or infringements, especially of rules.

torque: the movement of a force or system of forces, tending to cause rotation.

traverse: to pass or move over, along, or through.

Unlike the other motorcycle competitions, trials do not involve racing. Instead, trials are a test of the rider and his or her bike against specific elements of the terrain. Courses are strewn with an assortment of logs, boulders, and other similar obstacles. Riders attempt to clear, climb, **traverse,** or otherwise overcome the obstacle as designated without having their feet touch the ground or obstacle (known in the sport as "dabbing").

Scoring is on a point system. In trials, points are bad. They are awarded for **infractions** like touching the ground or obstacle, dismounting the bike altogether, rolling backward on an obstacle, or going out of bounds. There is no clock ticking against the rider in trials. Riders can take as much time as they want to complete all obstacles on the course, which are all within a designated boundary. Trials are about precision and control, not speed. The battle is between the rider and the course instead of directly against other riders.

Trials bikes are smaller than motocross or enduro machines and are designed to provide maximum **torque** rather than speed or power. They are also designed for the rider to stand while riding—they do not even have a seat at all.

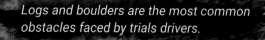

Logs and boulders are the most common obstacles faced by trials drivers.

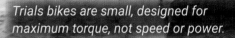

Trials bikes are small, designed for maximum torque, not speed or power.

Sidebar

The FIM Trial World Championship is the crown jewel of trials riding. There are indoor and outdoor versions. The outdoor version has existed in various forms since 1964, with the current version adopting its name in 1975. The indoor version is called the FIM X-Trial World Championship.

Spain is the most dominant nation in professional trials riding. Toni Bou of Spain won both the outdoor and indoor trial world titles in each year from 2007 to 2015, for a record nine straight double championships. His countrywoman Laia Sanz won the women's FIM Trial World Championship 13 times in 14 years between 2000 and 2013. Her only blemish was a second-place finish in 2007. Sanz is also a three-time women's FIM World Enduro Champion.

Text-Dependent Questions

1. What is dabbing?
2. How does scoring work in trials?
3. What are trials bikes designed to provide?

Research Project

Search the Internet for video of motorcycle trials competitions. Compile a list of the videos of the best trials performances, and examine what skills trials riders use versus racers.

Educational Video

Scan here for a view of some trials.

Off-Road Racing

The Baja 1000 runs through the Mexican desert between Ensenada and La Paz.

Words to Understand

booby trap: any hidden trap set for an unsuspecting person.

pinnacle: the highest or culminating point, as of success, power, fame, and so on.

primarily: essentially, mostly, chiefly, principally.

A truck spins its wheels during the 2013 Dakar Rally, one of the deadliest races in the world.

Auto sports have a long history of racing on something other than a paved surface. Many of the world's toughest races take place on the vast amount of rugged terrain found around the planet.

One of the toughest off-road races in the world is the Baja 1000. This race takes place annually in the deserts of Mexico, either in a loop starting and ending in Ensenada or going more than 1,000 miles (1,609 kilometers) from Ensenada to La Paz. The race is open to vehicles from motorcycles to 4x4 trucks and is especially notorious for having spectators **booby trap** the course.

The Dakar Rally is the world's most famous off-road race. For decades it was run from Paris, France, to Dakar, Senegal, in Africa. In 2005, 688 racers started the rally. The race moved to South America in 2009 due to security concerns along the African portion of the route that cancelled the 2008 race. The race is one of the deadliest for both spectators and racers. Twenty-eight racers and 42 spectators have been killed since the race started in 1979.

The World Rally Championship (WRC) is the **pinnacle** of international rally racing. In rally races, teams of drivers race from point to point over long distances in what is **primarily** an endurance challenge that often takes more than a day. In the WRC, the title goes to the driver with the most points after a season consisting of 14 rallies. The 2016 event had drivers racing on surfaces including snow, gravel, dirt, and pavement.

The Erzberg Rodeo is one of the toughest motorcycle races in the world. It is held on the side of an iron ore mine in Austria. The highlight of the 3-day event is the Hare Scramble, where 500 riders start the race at the base of the 35-kilometer (22 mile) course that goes straight up the side in the loose rock of the mine. In 2011, only nine riders were able to finish the race.

The World Rally Championship series takes drivers to diverse tracks and courses around the globe.

Sidebar

Honorable mention goes to Malaysia's Rainforest Challenge, a 4x4 truck race through the jungles of the South Asian nation during rainy season. Racers have 6 days to travel 500 miles (805 kilometers). For a race, the going is very slow at times. Due to the severe conditions, including torrential rain, floods, waist-deep mud, and landslides, it often takes hours to travel a single kilometer (half mile). Although all vehicles are equipped with winches, at the end of many stages, teams have been forced to abandon their trucks in the jungle and get help pulling them out the next day. The physical conditions are challenging for drivers as well, given the heat, humidity, and the constant presence of leeches and sand flies.

 Text-Dependent Questions

1. In what Mexican city does the Baja 1000 traditionally start?
2. How many rallies make up the WRC?
3. In what country is the Erzberg Rodeo held?

 **Research Project**

Do a report on the East African Safari Rally, including its history, number of entrants, distance, and so on. Be sure to include at least three interesting examples of race lore.

 Educational Video

Watch this video on off-road racing.

Want to Participate?

Check out some of these incredible places to either participate or watch these amazing all-terrain sports around the world.

Freestyle BMX:

Black Pearl Skate Park, Grand Cayman

Black Pearl is the planet's biggest outdoor skate park. This park has everything from the bowls vert riders are looking for to the rails, ledges, and stairs street riders crave.

Here are more great places to ride freestyle BMX:

Denver Skate Park, CO

This park has bowls of every size to suit every style. Street features abound, with banks, hips, and hubbas.

Mega Underground Bike Park, Louisville, KY

The biggest non-outdoor bike park in the world is actually 100 feet (30 meters) underground. Built in an abandoned limestone mine, Mega has 5 miles (8 kilometers) of trails and jumps.

Denver Skate Park, CO

Colorado Trail, CO

MTB:

Colorado Trail, CO

Rated at the intermediate skill level this 535-mile (861 kilometer) trail will be a test at elevation, but the views are spectacular. This is a single track, but it has lots of connecting trails.

Here are more great places to MTB:

Moab, UT

Here you will find the Whole Enchilada, 26 miles (42 kilometers) of trails that start at an elevation over 10,000 feet (3 kilometers). Technically diverse and mostly downhill, this advanced trail system ends at the Colorado River.

Kitchener, Canada

The Hydrocut is a fast-flowing single track through low-lying Canadian woods that can be completed in fewer than 2 hours.

Franz Josef, New Zealand

ATV:

Dar Azawad, Morocco
The terrain here is sand, sand, and more sand, as Dar Azawad is surrounded by the vast Sahara desert. Be sure to wear protective gear in the blistering North African heat.

Here are some more places to ride ATVs:
Winnsboro, SC
Carolina Adventure World is a dedicated ATV sanctuary, featuring varying terrain and trails for riders of all skill levels.

Franz Josef, New Zealand
This mountain village on the west coast of New Zealand's south island features amazing views along with miles of forest trails.

Motocross:

Glen Helen, SC
This track typically hosts the first or the last race of the AMA national schedule as it is one of the most challenging on the circuit. It features a 200-foot (61 meter) climb known as Mount St. Helen.

BMX:

Pietermaritzburg BMX Club, South Africa
This 380-meter (1,247 foot) track was custom built by world-renowned designer Tom Ritzehthaler for the 2010 UCI BMX World Championships. It has separate start ramps for advanced riders and is designed to force riders to strategically balance speed and power.

Here is another place to ride BMX:

Chula Vista BMX, CA
This facility is part of the training center for the U.S. Olympic team and features three state-of-the-art tracks.

Further Reading:

Loh-Hagan, Virginia. *Extreme BMX Freestyle (Nailed It!)*. 45th Parallel Press, 2015.

Maurer, Tracy. *ATV Racing (Super Speed)*. North Mankato, MN: Capstone Press, 2013

Schoenherr, Alicia. *Mountain Biking (Kids' Guides)*. North Mankato, MN: The Child's World Inc., 2014

Internet Resources:

USA BMX
https://www.usabmx.com/#&slider1=1

Score International Off-Road Racing
http://score-international.com/

Bicycling
http://www.bicycling.com/tags/mountain-bike

International Motorcycling Federation
http://www.fim-live.com/

Photo Credits:

Cover: homydesign/Shutterstock.com, ARENA Creative/Shutterstock.com, Weblogiq/Shutterstock.com, Maciej Kopaniecki; Page 3: Kineticimagery/Dreamstime.com; Page 6: Tosca Weijers/Dreamstime.com; Page 7: Zoltan Nagy/Dreamstime.com; Page 8: Maxim Petrichuk/Dreamstime.com; Page 9: Maxim Petrichuk/Dreamstime.com; Page 10: Maxim Petrichuk/Dreamstime.com; Page 11: Maxim Petrichuk/Dreamstime.com, Franant/Dreamstime.com; Page 12: Ukrphoto/Dreamstime.com; Page 13: Steirus/Dreamstime.com; Page 14: Jinfeng Zhang/Dreamstime.com; Page 15: Homydesign/Dreamstime.com, Dreamstime.com Agency; Page 16: One8mmedia/Dreamstime.com; Page 17: Homydesign/Dreamstime.com; Page 18: Massimiliano Leban/Dreamstime.com; Page 19: Bryan Culbertson/Dreamstime.com, Ron Sumners/Dreamstime.com; Page 20: 400ex127/Dreamstime.com; Page 21: Chris Hellyar/Dreamstime.com; Page 22: Aiisha/Dreamstime.com; Page 23: Paparazzofamily/Dreamstime.com, Zoltan Nagy/Dreamstime.com; Page 24: Anthony Aneese Totah Jr/Dreamstime.com; Page 25: Cia Pix/Dreamstime.com; Page 26: Maxim Petrichuk/Dreamstime.com; Page 27: Bryan Culbertson/Dreamstime.com, Jandrie Lombard/Dreamstime.com; Page 28: Toa555/Dreamstime.com; Page 29: Paparazzofamily/Dreamstime.com; Page 30: Paparazzofamily/Dreamstime.com; Page 31: Paparazzofamily/Dreamstime.com, Homydesign/Dreamstime.com; Page 32: Glennel Warren/Dreamstime.com; Page 33: Glennel Warren/Dreamstime.com; Page 34: I4lcocl2/Dreamstime.com; Page 35: I4lcocl2/Dreamstime.com; Page 36: Bflorky/Dreamstime.com; Page 37: Andres Rodriguez/Dreamstime.com; Page 38: Domenico Sechi/Dreamstime.com; Page 39: Konstantin Kowarsch/Dreamstime.com, Milan Kopcok/Dreamstime.com; Page 40: Xnatedawgx/Wikimedia Commons; Page 41: Hopkins.m.s/Wikimedia Commons; Page 42: Pseudopanax/Wikimedia Commons; Page 44: Peter Close/Dreamstime.com; Page 45: Neil Lockhart/Dreamstime.com; Page 46: Lasse Behnke/Dreamstime.com

Video Credits:

Mountain Biking - http://x-qr.net/1Hnf

BMX - http://x-qr.net/1H1i

Freestyle BMX - http://x-qr.net/1GSS

ATV - http://x-qr.net/1GLD

Motocross - http://x-qr.net/1Hc6

Enduro - http://x-qr.net/1GRT

Trials - http://x-qr.net/1GwF

Off-road Racing - http://x-qr.net/1HfY

Author Bio:

Andrew Luke is a former journalist, reporting on both sports and general news for many years at television stations in various locations across the United States affiliated with NBC, CBS, and Fox. Prior to his journalism career, he worked with the Boston Red Sox Major League baseball team. An avid writer and sports enthusiast, he has authored 11 other books on sports topics. In his downtime Andrew enjoys family time with his wife and two young children and attending hockey and baseball games in his home city of Pittsburgh, PA.

Index:

In this index, page numbers in bold italic font indicate photos or videos.